THE AVADA™
TREASURE HUNT
WORKBOOK

Experiencing of the Presence of God
Hearing His Word for You
Discovering His Will For Your Most Abundant Life

Companion Guide to
The AVADA™ Principle

Michael Sipe

Copyright 2019, Michael Sipe

All rights reserved. No part of this book may be used or reproduced by any means, graphic, electronic, or mechanical (including any information storage retrieval system) without the express written permission from the author, except in the case of brief quotations for use in articles and reviews wherein appropriate attribution of the source is made.

ISBN: 978-1-7334997-3-6 (Amazon Print)
ISBN: 978-1-7334997-4-3 (IngramSpark) PAPERBACK

For bulk purchase and for booking, contact:

AVADA Publishing Group
P.O. Box 5202
Bend, OR 97708
AVADAPublishing@gmail.com

Because of the dynamic nature of the Internet, web addresses or links contained in this book may have been changed since publication and may no longer be valid. The content of this book and all expressed opinions are those of the author and do not reflect the publisher or the publishing team. The author is solely responsible for all content included herein.

All Scripture quotations, unless otherwise indicated, are taken from the Holy Bible, New International Version®, NIV®. Copyright ©1973, 1978, 1984, 2011 by Biblica, Inc.™ Used by permission of Zondervan. All rights reserved worldwide. www.zondervan.com. The "NIV" and "New International Version" are trademarks registered in the United States Patent and Trademark Office by Biblica, Inc.™

Scripture quotations marked (AMPCE) are taken from the Amplified Bible, Copyright © 1954, 1958, 1962, 1964, 1965, 1987 by The Lockman Foundation. Used by permission.

Scripture quotations are from the ESV® Bible (The Holy Bible, English Standard Version®), copyright © 2001 by Crossway Bibles, a publishing ministry of Good News Publishers. Used by permission. All rights reserved.

Scripture quotations marked (NLT) are taken from the Holy Bible, New Living Translation, copyright ©1996, 2004, 2015 by Tyndale House Foundation. Used by permission of Tyndale House Publishers, Inc., Carol Stream, Illinois 60188. All rights reserved.

Scripture quotations marked (TLB) are taken from The Living Bible copyright © 1971. Used by permission of Tyndale House Publishers, Inc., Carol Stream, Illinois 60188. All rights reserved.

Scripture quotations marked MSG are taken from THE MESSAGE, copyright © 1993, 2002, 2018 by Eugene H. Peterson. Used by permission of NavPress. All rights reserved. Represented by Tyndale House Publishers, Inc.

Scripture quotations marked TPT are from The Passion Translation®. Copyright © 2017, 2018 by Passion & Fire Ministries, Inc. Used by permission. All rights reserved. ThePassionTranslation.com.

AVADA™ is a registered trademark with all rights reserved.

Companion Guide to the AVADA™ Principle available at Amazon.com:

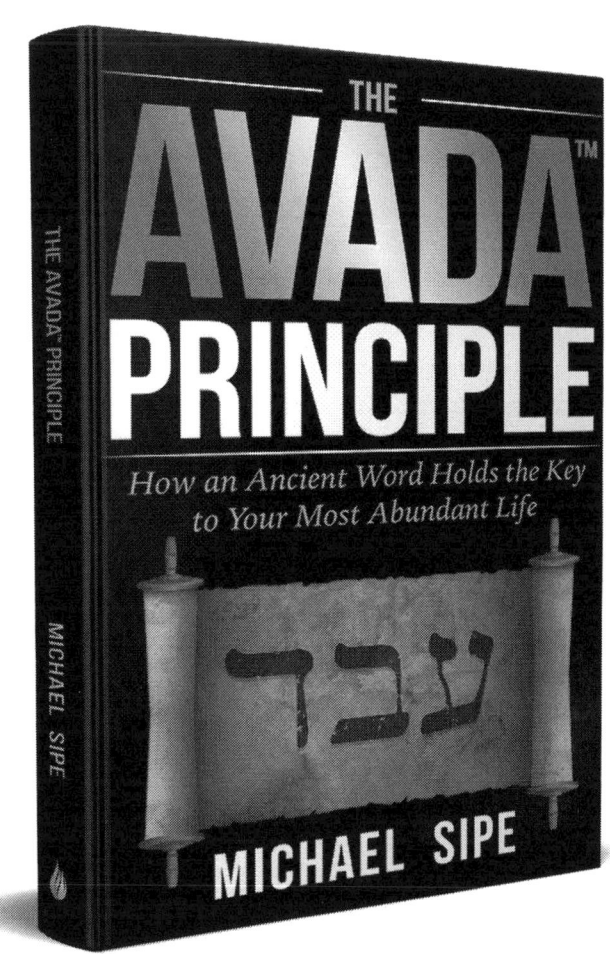

Table of Contents

Introduction	1
The AVADA Principle Overview	5
Approach and Methodology	9
Your AVADA Treasure Hunt	13
Example Treasure Hunt	18
A 30-Day Treasure Hunt	22
Conclusion	113
Additional Resources	115
About the Author	117

Your Treasure Hunt

"If you seek it like silver and search for it as for hidden treasures, then you will understand the fear of the Lord and find the knowledge of God."
—Proverbs 2: 4-5

"As for the rich in this present age, charge them not to be haughty, nor to set their hopes on the uncertainty of riches, but on God, who richly provides us with everything to enjoy. They are to do good, to be rich in good works, to be generous and ready to share, thus storing up treasure for themselves as a good foundation for the future, so that they may take hold of that which is truly life."
—1 Timothy 6: 17-19

"The kingdom of heaven is like treasure hidden in a field, which a man found and covered up. Then in his joy he goes and sells all that he has and buys that field."
—Matthew 13: 44 ESV

"I will give you the treasures of darkness and the hoards in secret places, that you may know that it is I, the Lord, the God of Israel, who call you by your name. For the sake of my servant Jacob, and Israel my chosen, I call you by your name, I name you, though you do not know me."
—Isaiah 45: 3-4

"For where your treasure is, there will your heart be also."
—Luke 12: 34 ESV

"And he said to them, 'Therefore every scribe who has been trained for the kingdom of heaven is like a master of a house, who brings out of his treasure what is new and what is old.'"
—Matthew 13: 52 ESV

"Blessed is the one who finds wisdom, and the one who gets understanding, for the gain from her is better than gain from silver and her profit better than gold. She is more precious than jewels, and nothing you desire can compare with her."
—Proverbs 3: 13-15 ESV

"Therefore, do not be anxious, saying, 'What shall we eat?' or 'What shall we drink?' or 'What shall we wear?' For the Gentiles seek after all these things, and your heavenly Father knows that you need them all. But seek first the kingdom of God and his righteousness, and all these things will be added to you."
—Matthew 6: 31-33

INTRODUCTION

Welcome to your AVADA Life Treasure Hunt Workbook. You're in for an amazing 30-day adventure! I've led Treasure Hunts for many leaders, individually and in small groups. <u>Every time</u>, the Presence of God is obvious and manifest. <u>Every time</u>, *every person* clearly hears from God. They know it and so does everyone else in the room. It is an incredibly powerful and emotional experience. Most of the time, the leaders I do this with are not what you would call "religious" or spiritual leaders. Usually, they are not vocational pastors or sophisticated Bible students, although the Treasure Hunt approach works for everyone. Typically, I work with marketplace leaders. These are highly accomplished men and women experiencing massive success in business. They are smart, practical, bottom line, "Show me the ROI!" types of leaders.

As they each engage in their Treasure Hunt, they are deeply moved – frequently to tears – as they experience the Presence of God and hear Him speak to them directly about <u>their</u> lives. I doubt there is anything more profoundly impactful than the moments when a man or woman personally experiences that God, the creator and ruler of the entire universe, loves them, cares specifically about their life and speaks to them individually. The second most profound experience is seeing that God loves <u>everyone</u> like that. It's amazing to watch people discover they are truly special…and so is everyone else.

Get ready. That's what's in store for you in these pages. I've organized the workbook to be used over a 30-day period. In that time, you'll prayerfully reflect and meditate on about 90-120 Scripture passages. 30 days is also a good timeframe to build new skills and habits. However, you can do this study over whatever period of time you like. Every single day's exercise will yield a revelation from God, regardless of whether you do thirty days in a row, or skip a few. I expect you'll experience more impact if you do the workbook over the course of a month, but frankly, since the whole objective of this study is to help you hear from God, if it takes you a year or a lifetime to complete each daily study…you win!

I wish I could be with you to personally share the adventure on which you're about to embark. I hope you'll write to us at **AVADAPublishing@gmail.com** and share your experiences and discoveries. I can hardly wait to hear what God has for you!

Purpose

The purpose of this workbook is to be a tool for you use to experience the Presence of God, hear directly from Him, and discover His will for your most abundant life.

You Can Hear From God

Do you believe you can hear from God? Do you believe you can hear from Him daily? Are you willing to believe you will hear from Him as you enter into the next 30 days of the AVADA Life Treasure Hunt? As Henry Ford said, "Whether you think you can or think you can't, you're right."

The truth is, God is speaking to you right now. He wants to speak to you as you use this workbook. If you are not hearing from God, it's not because God is the problem or because He is absent. It's probably due to one of these three causes:

1. **You are not Hearing because You are the Problem.**

   - You doubt that God speaks to people today…now…in this generation.
   - You don't believe He wants to speak to you and that He is speaking to you… even right now.
   - You don't believe you can hear Him.
   - You don't <u>want</u> to hear Him and what He has to say. Perhaps that is because:
     - You are afraid of God, or
     - Because you hold negative opinions about Him, or
     - You think you are unworthy of hearing from God, or
     - You think He will speak words of condemnation, or
     - You don't want to hear His words of conviction about an area of sin, because you don't want to change, or
     - You don't really want to hear God's truth, because you just want to do what you want to do.

- You talk too much and listen too little.
- You are attempting to impose your will on God, in essence telling Him what you want to hear.
- You are unwilling to seek Him. The excuses are rampant here and usually sound like, "I don't have the time or energy to seek God and to hear His voice."

Here is the truth: God said: *"If you look for me wholeheartedly, you will find me."* Jeremiah 29:13 NLT

This workbook is an opportunity for you to seek God with all your mind, will, heart and strength. Go for it. Expect to hear from God as you work through the exercise in this guide. He is faithful.

2. **You are not Hearing because God is Quiet.** You and I are not God, so we don't actually know why God seems to be silent sometimes. We know He did not go "away." He is always Present. But sometimes, even when we think we are seeking Him diligently, it seems He is quiet. Here are some speculations for why God might be silent. They are just possibilities for your consideration.

- God wants you to do what He already told you to do before He gives you more instructions.
- God wants you to seek Him more fervently. There is much to be learned in the seeking and the waiting.
- God wants you to learn something else first before answering your current question.
- God's timing is different than yours. And superior to yours.
- You are the problem. See point one above.

When God seems quiet, ask <u>Him</u> why. I don't know.

3. **You are not Hearing because You Don't Know How to Seek His Presence.** This can be a legitimate issue for "regular" people. Vocational pastors invest years in schooling and study and devote their lives to learning how to hear from God. But there's a good chance that you might not have had the opportunity to learn how to hear from God. If so, allow this workbook to be an introduction to hearing from God and the greatest adventure possible:

A life lived daily in the Power and Presence of God, hearing from Him moment by moment as you embrace an AVADA Life.

The AVADA™ Principle Overview

The *AVADA™ Principle* book is the result of my search of the Bible for the key to an abundant life. It's an exploration of the conceptual richness of the answer I found, which lies in an ancient Hebrew word that shows up at the very beginning of the Bible. Although the word exists only in the Hebrew versions of the Old Testament, the concepts captured in this one word are woven throughout the entire Old and New Testaments. It is so central to the overall message of the Bible that I call it a **principle**.

That word is avodah. It's a word that simultaneously means work, worship and service. From this word, I coined the contemporary term AVADA™. In the book, as we examine the roots of this ancient word and take a deep dive into the true meanings of work, worship and service, the AVADA Principle will become evident. I make the case that avodah can be interpreted and understood to mean God's covenant that His very Spirit is breathed into an integrated life of work, worship, and service. In living an AVADA Life we have the privilege of more fully enjoying God's hand of favor, experiencing His presence, His power and His blessing every day.

In a nutshell, that's the AVADA Principle. Live an integrated life of work, worship, and service, and enjoy God's hand of favor. Enjoy His power. Enjoy the breath of His Holy Spirit infusing your life. Enjoy hearing, "Well done!" every day. Enjoy a life filled with abundance and God's highest and best. I want that. I bet you do too.

The AVADA Principle is not complicated. That's one of the main characteristics of a principle. It's not complicated. It's just a fundamental truth and rule of conduct. We can't fight a principle. It's a make-or-break choice. We either embrace a principle, and it makes us, or we resist it, and it breaks us.

However, just because a principle like the AVADA Principle is not complicated, that does not necessarily make it easy to embrace. Therefore, you're probably asking, as I did, "What would an AVADA Life look like?" Fortunately, the Bible has a wonderful answer to that question. The Apostle Paul lays it out beautifully for us in the Book of Romans in the New Testament:

"So, here's what I want you to do, God helping you: Take your everyday, ordinary life - your sleeping, eating, going-to-work, and walking-around life - and place it before God as an offering. Embracing what God does for you is the best thing you can do for him. Don't become so well-adjusted to your culture that you fit into it without even thinking. Instead, fix your attention on God. You'll be changed from the inside out. Readily recognize what he wants from you, and quickly respond to it. Unlike the culture around you, always dragging you down to its level of immaturity, God brings the best out of you, develops well-formed maturity in you.

"I'm speaking to you out of deep gratitude for all that God has given me, and especially as I have responsibilities in relation to you. Living then, as every one of you does, in pure grace, it's important that you not misinterpret yourselves as people who are bringing this goodness to God. No, God brings it all to you. The only accurate way to understand ourselves is by what God is and by what he does for us, not by what we are and what we do for him.

"In this way, we are like the various parts of a human body. Each part gets its meaning from the body as a whole, not the other way around. The body we're talking about is Christ's body of chosen people. Each of us finds our meaning and function as a part of his body. But as a chopped-off finger or cut-off toe, we wouldn't amount to much, would we? So, since we find ourselves fashioned into all these excellently formed and marvelously functioning parts in Christ's body, let's just go ahead and be what we were made to be, without enviously or pridefully comparing ourselves with each other, or trying to be something we aren't. If you preach, just preach God's Message, nothing else; if you help, just help, don't take over; if you teach, stick to your teaching; if you give encouraging guidance, be careful that you don't get bossy; if you're put in charge, don't manipulate; if you're called to give aid to people in distress, keep your eyes open and be quick to respond; if you work with the disadvantaged, don't let yourself get irritated with them or depressed by them. Keep a smile on your face.

"Love from the center of who you are; don't fake it. Run for dear life from evil; hold on for dear life to good. Be good friends who love deeply; practice playing second fiddle. Don't burn out; keep yourselves fueled and aflame. Be alert servants of the Master, cheerfully expectant. Don't quit in hard times; pray all the harder. Help needy Christians; be inventive in hospitality. Bless your enemies; no cursing under your breath. Laugh with your happy friends when they're happy; share

tears when they're down. Get along with each other; don't be stuck-up. Make friends with nobodies; don't be the great somebody. Don't hit back; discover beauty in everyone. If you've got it in you, get along with everybody. Don't insist on getting even; that's not for you to do. 'I'll do the judging,' says God. 'I'll take care of it.'

"Our Scriptures tell us that if you see your enemy hungry, go buy that person lunch, or if he's thirsty, get him a drink. Your generosity will surprise him with goodness. Don't let evil get the best of you; get the best of evil by doing good." Romans 12 MSG

To me, this version of Romans 12 epitomizes the AVADA Life.

For many years, I have appreciated the perspectives offered in the following quote. It's been attributed to L.P. Jacks, to the author James Michener, to an anonymous Zen master, and simply to the ubiquitous "Anonymous." Regardless of its source, we can work with the approach to life it describes as an entry point into a growing understanding of an AVADA Life:

"A master in the art of living makes little distinction between his work and his play, his labor and his leisure, his mind and his body, his education and his recreation, his love and his religion. He hardly knows which is which. He simply pursues his vision of excellence at whatever he does, leaving others to decide whether he is working or playing. To him, he is always doing both."

Applied to the pursuit of an AVADA Life, it might read like this:

"Students of AVADA living make little distinction between our work and our play, our labor and our leisure, our work and our worship, our worship and our recreation, our worship and our service, our service and our work. We hardly know which is which. We embrace an integrated life and pursue our Spirit-inspired vision of excellence at whatever we do, leaving others to decide whether we are working, playing, worshiping or serving. As for us, we are simply saying yes to all that God has for us and going for His highest and best in all that we do."

At its essence, in an AVADA Life, you desire, receive, embrace, experience, enjoy, and delight in the Presence and Power of God in every aspect of your life - 24 hours a day, seven days a week, 365 days a year for the rest of your life and forever.

An AVADA Life flows out of a special perspective, viewpoint, and mindset. But it's more than a mindset; it's a way of <u>acting</u> out of that mindset. With that as a backdrop,

The AVADA™ Principle unpacks the avodah concept and explores how you and I can live a modern day AVADA Life… an integrated and harmonious life of work, worship, and service that is pleasing to God and filled with His Power and Presence.

I urge you to read *The AVADA™ Principle* before you plunge into this Workbook. Everything will go better as you grasp the depth, richness and potential of an AVADA Life.

However, just <u>reading</u> about an AVADA Life doesn't get you to actually <u>living</u> an AVADA Life. That's why I created this Workbook, so God can coach you and guide you into the AVADA Life He has for you. Let's get started.

Approach and Methodology

There are many ways to seek God and many approaches to Bible study and devotional time. This workbook takes a customized approach intended to help you prayerfully hear what God has to say to you about how He wants <u>you</u> to live an AVADA Life. It is derived and adapted for our purposes here from five approaches to Bible study, which are all incorporated into the methodology I'm suggesting for your 30 days of reflections:

➢ **Word Study.** Word study approaches involve selection of a word, such as "Work." Then the origin, original meaning and use of the word "Work" in Scripture are investigated. Word studies are based on the original Biblical language. They involve use of a good study Bible, a Bible dictionary, exhaustive concordances, Bible commentaries, and often extensive online and published background research. Comprehensive word studies can take hours. They can take days, weeks or months. *The AVADA Principle* book is the result of my investigation into the words: Work, Worship and Service. This led me to the original Hebrew word "avad" and its derivations and forms. Thus, this Workbook has its start in a word study, but it is not in itself a word study. Obviously, you can spend as long as you like seeking God and prayerfully meditating on His Word. However, a Treasure Hunt is premised on about 30 minutes of study, prayer and journaling each morning.

➢ **Topical Study.** With topical studies, you pick a topic, such as "God's Faithfulness," and you consider every verse in the Bible on that topic. This can take a long time, depending on the topic. Topical studies involve not only the Bible, but a Bible dictionary, exhaustive concordances, commentaries, online tools and outside research. *The AVADA Principle* book is the result of my study of the topics: Work,

Worship and Service. Thus, this Treasure Hunt Workbook has its start in a topical study, but it is not in itself a topical study. The topics selected for the entire workbook are Work, Worship and Service. Again, it's intended that each day's reflections can be accomplished in about 30 minutes.

- **Textual Study.** With textual study, you start with a particular passage, make your own individual observations, consider the applications for your life and pray for God's guidance and insights on the selected text. This is the format of the popular SOAP Bible study introduced originally by Wayne Cordiero, currently chancellor of New Hope Christian College in Eugene, OR. SOAP stands for Scripture, Observation, Application and Prayer. Pastor Cordiero is the author of the Life Journal, which is used by thousands of churches worldwide, and which is available at **https://www.liferesources.cc/journaling**. I have used the SOAP methodology for many years and highly recommend it. Although I have incorporated part of this approach into the Treasure Hunt methodology, this Workbook is not a SOAP study.

- **Lectio Divina.** *Lectio Divina* means "divine reading" in Latin. It's a method that dates back to the 3rd century for studying Scripture and hearing from God that combines Scripture reading with prayer and meditation. It involves reading a Scripture passage, praying about it, meditating on it and contemplating it. The purpose of *lectio devina* is not gaining "head knowledge." It does not involve seeking external input from the writings or teachings of other men or women; thus, no commentaries or outside resources are required (or appropriate). Although there are plenty of times we should be willing to learn from the teachings of other people, as 1 Timothy 2:5 says, "Jesus is the only mediator between man and God."

Lectio Divina seeks the <u>direct wisdom of God</u> resident in Scripture. It's about communion with God and hearing from the Holy Spirit in the context of Scripture.

According to Ruth Haley Barton in her book *Sacred Rhythms: Arranging Our Lives for Spiritual Transformation,* "We need a way of approaching Scripture that will move us very concretely from our overreliance on information-gathering to an <u>experience</u> of Scripture as a place of intimate encounter." "…the practice of *lectio divina* is rooted in the belief that through the presence of the Holy Spirit, the Scriptures are indeed alive and active as we engage them for spiritual transformation (Hebrews 4:12)."

An AVADA Treasure Hunt is an application of *lectio divina*, especially with its focus on engaging with the Holy Spirit and allowing the Spirit to direct and inform our Scripture selection and our reading and reflection. All you need for this method of study is a half hour, the willingness to calm yourself, a desire to hear from God, a good cross-reference Bible and a journal.

➢ **Abiding.** In addition to the methods above, all of which informed the design of the AVADA Treasure Hunt, I also want to acknowledge the impact a few years ago that Rich Case and his Abiding Class had on my approach to Bible study. I recommend this class and Rich's teaching highly. Visit **https://allforjesus.today** for more information.

Your AVADA Treasure Hunt

An AVADA Treasure Hunt is a custom blend of all the above approaches designed to help you prayerfully hear what God has to say to you specifically about how He wants you to live an AVADA Life. Here's how it works. An example follows the instructions.

Resources Needed:

1. **Bible.** You'll need a good paper reference Bible – not an Internet or electronic Bible. Use an actual paper Bible in a well-established translation like NIV, ESV, NKJV or KJV. Do not use a paraphrase version like the Message. Your Bible should have cross-references in the center or side margins so you can do a cross-reference study.

2. **The AVADA Treasure Hunt Workbook.**

3. **Journal (Optional).** You may want to extract thoughts from this Workbook and transfer them to your regular journal. Also, you may find that you want to write more extensively on the studies than the Workbook space allows.

4. **3"x5" Index Cards or Sticky Notes.** Purchase a standard deck of 3"x5" note cards or sticky notes to use as a daily reminder of your prayers for the day. Alternatively, you could make notes in your daily paper planner. Or make notes and set up reminders at the end of your study session in your digital calendar.

5. **Pen or pencil.**

6. **A Quiet Space.** Please leave your cellphone, tablet and computer in another room to avoid distraction.

7. **Music (Optional).** I like to study with soft instrumental worship music in the background. Piano and guitar work well for me. I suggest you try this as well. It will set the mood for your study. Personally, I find music with lyrics to be distracting. Do what works for you.

8. **30 Minutes.** You can do a daily Treasure Hunt in as little as 30 minutes. Obviously if you want to spend more time in God's Word than 30 minutes a day, that works too.

9. **Mindset.** Bring an open heart, an inquiring mind and a desire to seek the Lord.

10. **Expectancy.** Bring a sense of positive expectancy and a spirit of anticipation for your conversation with God and for the discoveries ahead.

What you <u>don't need</u> is a computer, a tablet, a cell phone, a pile of additional reference materials and a bunch of distractions. Keep it simple. The point of the Treasure Hunt is discovering what God wants you to see in the Scriptures you read.

Process

1. **Put Your Spirit in the Lead.** An AVADA Life is a Spirit-led life. A Treasure Hunt connects your spirit with the Holy Spirit, so that you can hear directly from God as you read His Word. At any moment in time, some part of your body, soul or spirit is leading. Your body <u>should not</u> be in charge during a Treasure Hunt, so make yourself comfortable for 30 minutes. Your soul (mind, will, heart, emotions and conscience) <u>should not</u> be in charge during a Treasure Hunt. <u>Your spirit should be in the lead</u>. You must choose which part of you is in the lead. Otherwise, whichever part is the noisiest will lead. Your spirit is never noisy or intrusive. Therefore, it must be deliberately and consciously called into the lead, otherwise your restless body or mind or your emotions or another part of your soul will lead by default. Calling your spirit into the lead is very simple. Just do it. Pray a simple prayer like this before you start each Treasure Hunt:

"I bless my spirit and I call it into the lead and grant it spiritual authority over my body and soul as I enter into this time with God and His Word."

For more on this, read *Blessing Your Spirit* by Arthur Burk and Sylvia Gunter.

It's common for people to resist saying this little prayer. They say it's silly, foolish, unnecessary or too simple to be of much use. This Workbook is not the forum to argue the point. Here's my suggestion. Test the premise before you resist. Open a few days of Treasure Hunt with the "simple, silly and foolish" spirit blessing prayer. If you're not convinced then, try doing a Treasure Hunt with your body or soul in command. I bet you go back to saying the spirit blessing prayer and putting your spirit in the lead.

2. **Go to the Day's Worksheet.** Fill in the date and the Praise and Gratitude Prompts.

3. **Go to Your Bible.** Make sure you are using a paper Bible with <u>center or side margin cross references</u>. Go to the verse for the day noted in the Workbook. Write it in your Workbook in the space provided. Prayerfully reflect on the verse. Ask God questions like: "What are you trying to show me here? What do you want me to take away from this verse today? What does this reveal to me about your character? What does this verse show me about what you have done, what you are doing now or that you promise to do? Are there conditions to your promise? (If I _____, then you will _____) How am I supposed to respond? What am I supposed to do?"

    Ask God the AVADA questions: What do you want me to see here about Work? About Worship? About Service?

4. **Be Quiet and Wait.** Wait long enough in a posture of listening for God to respond. He may not. Or you might not "hear" Him. If so, you might want to review the beginning of this Workbook and reflect on why that might be. Perhaps this initial verse is only the starting point in your Treasure Hunt, and He does not have something for you in this verse. That's OK. Often your Treasure will be found not at the beginning of the search, but rather in the process of hunting. Perhaps He'll have an insight for you about the starting verse. Sometimes your Treasure for the day is in the very first verse, and in that case, your day's study will be complete. Otherwise, you'll need to search a bit more. You'll know. Just be quiet, ponder the verse and wait.

5. **Journal.** Write down what you see and hear out of the starting verse in the Workbook and/or in your personal journal. If you get nothing, that's OK. If you only get a little, that's OK. If all you get is the prompt to keep looking, that's OK. Whatever you write, don't over-work it. Don't over-spiritualize it. You're not

writing a novel or a Biblical commentary. Don't go outside your Bible for more references or external perspectives. Just jot down what God brings you. It's not a performance. It's not a contest. It's just your notes from a daily chat with God.

6. **Cross-Reference.** If you get something from the initial verse (or if you don't), when God indicates you should move on, then look at the scriptures referenced next to the starting verse. Ask God to highlight one. Don't agonize over this or force the choice, or pick a verse just because you might recognize it. Ask God to highlight where He wants you to go. He will. Don't negotiate or push back; simply go to that next verse. (See the Example for more clarification on this.) Write it down in the space provided. Meditate on it and ask God what He wants to highlight in the verse for you using the questions in the Workbook.

7. **Repeat.** Do steps 3 through 6 above until God says to stop. (See the Example for more clarification on this.)

8. **Summarize.** Write a short summary of what God has shown you – capture the "Treasure(s)" you found – in the Workbook and/or your journal. Consider asking a few additional confirming questions: "Do I <u>believe</u> what these verses say? Really? Why or why not? Do I feel a sense of struggle or conviction when I read the verses? How do these verses apply to my life situation? How is God revealing His general and specific will? What is He calling me to?"

9. **Share.** Share what God revealed in your Treasure Hunt with someone you care about and who has the character and perspective to receive it reverently and discuss it meaningfully. Invite them to get their own Workbook and do their own Treasure Hunts, either simultaneously with you or separately. You will both be profoundly impacted by the experience.

10. **Pray.** Pray specifically. Based on what you just read, what you heard in the Spirit and what you wrote in your journal, ask God to help you apply what He showed you. Ask Him to deliver and fulfill His revealed promises for you, your life, your business, your family and your community.

11. **Declarations.** Declarations are powerful tools to shape your AVADA Life. Declarations are emphatic statements about how things are and how things will be in your life. Jot down the declarations you have based on what God has revealed to you in your Treasure Hunt.

12. Daily Reminders. As you close your Treasure Hunt time, jot down your prayer reminders and key points for daily reflection on a note card or sticky note to refer to during the day. Consider scheduling a reminder in your calendar to pray at mid-morning, noon and mid-afternoon. Maybe even set digital alarms. In order for us to live an integrated life we need to actually integrate work, worship and service into each day. That takes intentionality and putting reminders in place is a simple way to keep God top of mind.

Example AVADA Treasure Hunt.

Let's take a look at an example Treasure Hunt so you can see what it looks like.

Before you turn the page, open your cross-referenced paper Bible to Matthew 13:44, which is the verse that launches the example, and follow along with me in a recent Treasure Hunt, as I start at Matthew 13:44, and then God takes me to Philippians 3:7,8. Note the center reference in the image below and find it in your Bible. After Philippians 3:7,8, God led me to Romans 10:15-13, which is the final verse He highlighted for my reflections that day. That day I was complete with only three verses. Some days the hunt continues through more verses. Each day is different.

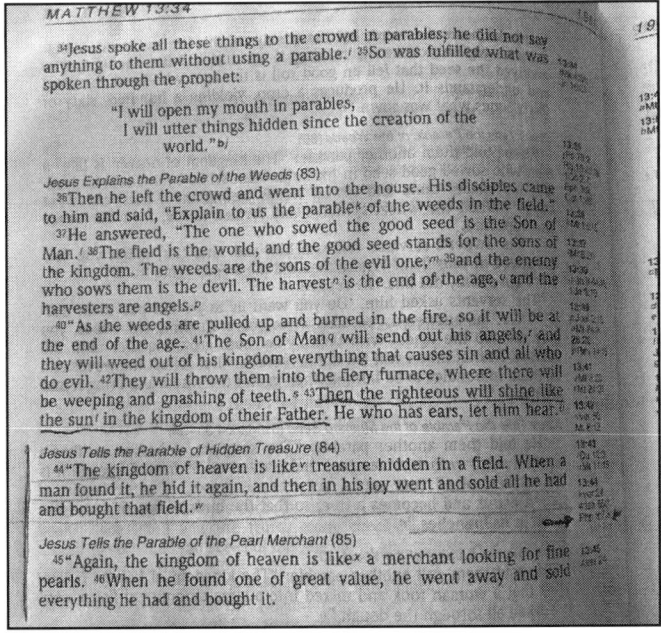
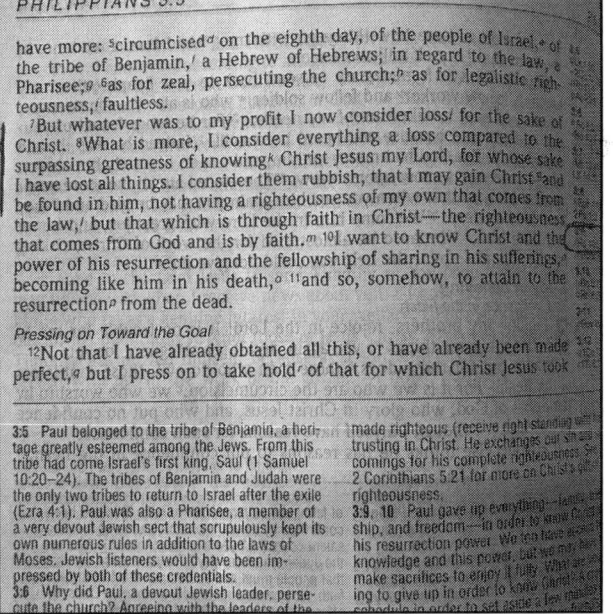

Michael Sipe

AVADA Treasure Hunt

Example. **Date:** September 18, 2019

"I bless my spirit and I call it into the lead and grant it spiritual authority over my body and soul as I enter into this time with God and His Word."

I Praise God today for: The beauty of the dawn today on the Cascade Range out my window.

I Thank God today for: Continued healing of my shoulder injury. Good health.

1. Prayerfully Reflect on Today's Opening Verse: Matthew 13:44

The kingdom of heaven is like treasure hidden in a field. When a man found it, he hid it again, and then in his joy went and sold all he had and bought that field.

What God is showing me in this Scripture:

About Work: Be willing to trade the work of a lifetime for true wealth. Treasure beyond compare.

About Worship: Go all in. There is joy in the exchange of my wealth for His wealth. The return is beyond my imagining.

About Service: Nothing today.

In General: I have to look for treasure. I have to be aware when I find it. I have to ACT in order to have the treasure in my life.

2. What Cross Reference Verse is God highlighting now? Philippians 3:7,8

But whatever was to my profit I now consider loss for the sake of Christ. What is more, I consider everything a loss compared to the surpassing greatness of knowing Christ Jesus my Lord, for whose sake I have lost all things. I consider them rubbish that I may gain Christ.

Prayerfully consider this new verse. What God is showing me in this Scripture:

About Work: *I want to work, to invest my life energy toward what matters eternally – relationship with you Lord.*

About Worship: *I will worship the Creator…not created things.*

About Service: *In your service Lord I am willing to sacrifice the things of this world.*

In General: *I want to be captivated by a relationship, not captured by stuff.*

3. What Cross Reference Verse is God highlighting now? Romans 10:5-13

If you openly declare that Jesus is Lord and believe in your heart that God raised him from the dead, you will be saved. For it is by believing in your heart that you are made right with God, and it is by openly declaring your faith that you are saved. As the Scriptures tell us, "Anyone who trusts in him will never be disgraced." Jew and Gentile are the same in this respect. They have the same Lord, who gives generously to all who call on him. For "Everyone who calls on the name of the Lord will be saved."

Prayerfully consider this new verse. What God is showing me in this Scripture:

About Work: *I want to do the work of sharing this good news.*

About Worship: *I will offer up a sacrifice of praise.*

About Service: *Sharing the good news is the ultimate act of love and the ultimate act of service to others.*

In General: *Done for today. Thank you Lord for these words!*

4. What Cross Reference Verse is God highlighting now? *(Nothing for today.)*

Prayerfully consider this new verse. What God is showing me in this Scripture:

About Work: _____

About Worship: _____

About Service: _____

In General: _____

5. What Cross Reference Verse is God highlighting now? *(Nothing for today.)*

Prayerfully consider this new verse. What God is showing me in this Scripture:

About Work: _____

About Worship: _____

About Service: _____

In General: _____

Summarize Today's Treasure(s). What God revealed to me about Work, Worship, Service and an integrated AVADA Life:

The ultimate Treasure is relationship with Christ...forever.

Today's Declarations: *I am a messenger of good news. I help people find the Treasure beyond all measure.*

Today's Prayer(s): *Lord, help me see and seize opportunities to share about the Treasure of knowing you. Help me do it in a winsome way that draws people to you.*

When and how will I remind myself today? *Sticky note on my computer: "I know where the Treasure is!"*

Additional Notes:

AVADA Treasure Hunt

Day One. **Date:** _____

"I bless my spirit and I call it into the lead and grant it spiritual authority over my body and soul as I enter into this time with God and His Word."

I Praise God today for: _____

I Thank God today for: _____

1. Prayerfully Reflect on Today's Opening Verse: Romans 12:1-2

_____

_____

_____

What God is showing me in this Scripture:

About Work: _____

About Worship: _____

About Service: _____

In General: _____

2. What Cross Reference Verse is God highlighting now? _____

_____

_____

_____

Prayerfully consider this new verse. What God is showing me in this Scripture:

About Work: _____

About Worship: _____

About Service: _____

In General: _____

3. What Cross Reference Verse is God highlighting now? _____

_____

_____

_____

Prayerfully consider this new verse. What God is showing me in this Scripture:

About Work: _____

About Worship: _____

About Service: _____

In General: _____

4. What Cross Reference Verse is God highlighting now? _____

_____

_____

_____

Prayerfully consider this new verse. What God is showing me in this Scripture:

About Work: _____

About Worship: _____

About Service: _____

In General: _____

Summarize Today's Treasure(s): _____

_____

_____

_____

_____

_____

Today's Declarations: _____

Today's Prayer: _____

When and how will I remind myself today? _____

Additional Notes:

AVADA Treasure Hunt

Day Two. **Date:** _____

"I bless my spirit and I call it into the lead and grant it spiritual authority over my body and soul as I enter into this time with God and His Word."

I Praise God today for: _____

I Thank God today for: _____

1. Prayerfully Reflect on Today's Opening Verse: Matthew 6:25-34

_____
_____
_____

What God is showing me in this Scripture:

About Work: _____

About Worship: _____

About Service: _____

In General: _____

2. What Cross Reference Verse is God highlighting now? _____

_____
_____
_____

Prayerfully consider this new verse. What God is showing me in this Scripture:

About Work: _____

About Worship: _____

About Service: _____

In General: _____

3. What Cross Reference Verse is God highlighting now? _____

_____

_____

_____

Prayerfully consider this new verse. What God is showing me in this Scripture:

About Work: _____

About Worship: _____

About Service: _____

In General: _____

4. What Cross Reference Verse is God highlighting now? _____

_____

_____

_____

Prayerfully consider this new verse. What God is showing me in this Scripture:

About Work: _____

About Worship: _____

About Service: _____

In General: _____

Summarize Today's Treasure(s): _____

_____

_____

_____

_____

_____

Today's Declarations: _____

Today's Prayer: _____

When and how will I remind myself today? _____

Additional Notes:

AVADA TREASURE HUNT

Day Three. **Date:** _____

"I bless my spirit and I call it into the lead and grant it spiritual authority over my body and soul as I enter into this time with God and His Word."

I Praise God today for: _____

I Thank God today for: _____

1. Prayerfully Reflect on Today's Opening Verse: John 14:6,12-17

_____
_____
_____

What God is showing me in this Scripture:

About Work: _____

About Worship: _____

About Service: _____

In General: _____

2. What Cross Reference Verse is God highlighting now? _____

_____
_____
_____

Prayerfully consider this new verse. What God is showing me in this Scripture:

About Work: _____

About Worship: _____

About Service: _____

In General: _____

3. What Cross Reference Verse is God highlighting now? _____

_____

_____

_____

Prayerfully consider this new verse. What God is showing me in this Scripture:

About Work: _____

About Worship: _____

About Service: _____

In General: _____

4. What Cross Reference Verse is God highlighting now? _____

_____

_____

_____

Prayerfully consider this new verse. What God is showing me in this Scripture:

About Work: _____

About Worship: _____

About Service: _____

In General: _____

Summarize Today's Treasure(s): _____

_____

_____

_____

_____

_____

Today's Declarations: _____

Today's Prayer: _____

When and how will I remind myself today? _____

Additional Notes:

AVADA Treasure Hunt

Day Four. Date: _____

*"I bless my spirit and I call it into the lead and grant it spiritual authority over
my body and soul as I enter into this time with God and His Word."*

I Praise God today for: _____

I Thank God today for: _____

1. Prayerfully Reflect on Today's Opening Verse: Colossians 3:17

_____

_____

_____

What God is showing me in this Scripture:

About Work: _____

About Worship: _____

About Service: _____

In General: _____

2. What Cross Reference Verse is God highlighting now? _____

_____

_____

_____

Prayerfully consider this new verse. What God is showing me in this Scripture:

About Work: _____

About Worship: _____

About Service: _____

In General: _____

3. What Cross Reference Verse is God highlighting now? _____

_____

_____

Prayerfully consider this new verse. What God is showing me in this Scripture:

About Work: _____

About Worship: _____

About Service: _____

In General: _____

4. What Cross Reference Verse is God highlighting now? _____

_____

_____

Prayerfully consider this new verse. What God is showing me in this Scripture:

About Work: _____

About Worship: _____

About Service: _____

In General: _____

Summarize Today's Treasure(s): _____

_____

_____

_____

_____

Today's Declarations: _____

Today's Prayer: _____

When and how will I remind myself today? _____

Additional Notes:

AVADA Treasure Hunt

Day Five.   **Date:** _____

"I bless my spirit and I call it into the lead and grant it spiritual authority over my body and soul as I enter into this time with God and His Word."

I Praise God today for: _____

I Thank God today for: _____

1. Prayerfully Reflect on Today's Opening Verse: John 10:7-15

_____

_____

_____

What God is showing me in this Scripture:

About Work: _____

About Worship: _____

About Service: _____

In General: _____

2. What Cross Reference Verse is God highlighting now? _____

_____

_____

_____

Prayerfully consider this new verse. What God is showing me in this Scripture:

About Work: _____

About Worship: _____

About Service: _____

In General: _____

3. What Cross Reference Verse is God highlighting now? _____

_____

_____

Prayerfully consider this new verse. What God is showing me in this Scripture:

About Work: _____

About Worship: _____

About Service: _____

In General: _____

4. What Cross Reference Verse is God highlighting now? _____

_____

_____

Prayerfully consider this new verse. What God is showing me in this Scripture:

About Work: _____

About Worship: _____

About Service: _____

In General: _____

Summarize Today's Treasure(s): _____

_____

_____

_____

_____

_____

Today's Declarations: _____

Today's Prayer: _____

When and how will I remind myself today? _____

Additional Notes:

AVADA Treasure Hunt

Day Six.   **Date:** _____

"I bless my spirit and I call it into the lead and grant it spiritual authority over my body and soul as I enter into this time with God and His Word."

I Praise God today for: _____

I Thank God today for: _____

1. Prayerfully Reflect on Today's Opening Verse: Romans 6:15-23

_____

_____

_____

What God is showing me in this Scripture:

About Work: _____

About Worship: _____

About Service: _____

In General: _____

2. What Cross Reference Verse is God highlighting now? _____

_____

_____

_____

Prayerfully consider this new verse. What God is showing me in this Scripture:

About Work: _____

About Worship: _____

About Service: _____

In General: _____

3. What Cross Reference Verse is God highlighting now? _____

_____

_____

_____

Prayerfully consider this new verse. What God is showing me in this Scripture:

About Work: _____

About Worship: _____

About Service: _____

In General: _____

4. What Cross Reference Verse is God highlighting now? _____

_____

_____

_____

Prayerfully consider this new verse. What God is showing me in this Scripture:

About Work: _____

About Worship: _____

About Service: _____

In General: _____

Summarize Today's Treasure(s): _____

_____

_____

_____

_____

_____

Today's Declarations: _____

Today's Prayer: _____

When and how will I remind myself today? _____

Additional Notes:

AVADA Treasure Hunt

Day Seven. **Date:** _____

"I bless my spirit and I call it into the lead and grant it spiritual authority over my body and soul as I enter into this time with God and His Word."

I Praise God today for: _____

I Thank God today for: _____

1. Prayerfully Reflect on Today's Opening Verse: Genesis 3:17-19

_____
_____
_____

What God is showing me in this Scripture:

About Work: _____

About Worship: _____

About Service: _____

In General: _____

2. What Cross Reference Verse is God highlighting now? _____

_____
_____
_____

Prayerfully consider this new verse. What God is showing me in this Scripture:

About Work: _____

About Worship: _____

About Service: _____

In General: _____

3. What Cross Reference Verse is God highlighting now? _____

_____

_____

_____

Prayerfully consider this new verse. What God is showing me in this Scripture:

About Work: _____

About Worship: _____

About Service: _____

In General: _____

4. What Cross Reference Verse is God highlighting now? _____

_____

_____

_____

Prayerfully consider this new verse. What God is showing me in this Scripture:

About Work: _____

About Worship: _____

About Service: _____

In General: _____

Summarize Today's Treasure(s): _____

_____

_____

_____

_____

_____

Today's Declarations: _____

Today's Prayer: _____

When and how will I remind myself today? _____

Additional Notes:

AVADA Treasure Hunt

Day Eight.   **Date:** _____

*"I bless my spirit and I call it into the lead and grant it spiritual authority over
my body and soul as I enter into this time with God and His Word."*

I Praise God today for: _____

I Thank God today for: _____

1. Prayerfully Reflect on Today's Opening Verse: John 5:19-23

_____
_____
_____

What God is showing me in this Scripture:

About Work: _____

About Worship: _____

About Service: _____

In General: _____

2. What Cross Reference Verse is God highlighting now? _____

_____
_____
_____

Prayerfully consider this new verse. What God is showing me in this Scripture:

About Work: _____

About Worship: _____

About Service: _____

In General: _____

3. What Cross Reference Verse is God highlighting now? _____

_____

_____

_____

Prayerfully consider this new verse. What God is showing me in this Scripture:

About Work: _____

About Worship: _____

About Service: _____

In General: _____

4. What Cross Reference Verse is God highlighting now? _____

_____

_____

_____

Prayerfully consider this new verse. What God is showing me in this Scripture:

About Work: _____

About Worship: _____

About Service: _____

In General: _____

Summarize Today's Treasure(s): _____

_____

_____

_____

_____

_____

Today's Declarations: _____

Today's Prayer: _____

When and how will I remind myself today? _____

Additional Notes:

AVADA Treasure Hunt

Day Nine.   **Date:** _____

"I bless my spirit and I call it into the lead and grant it spiritual authority over my body and soul as I enter into this time with God and His Word."

I Praise God today for: _____

I Thank God today for: _____

1. Prayerfully Reflect on Today's Opening Verse: Isaiah 55:8-11

_____
_____
_____

What God is showing me in this Scripture:

About Work: _____

About Worship: _____

About Service: _____

In General: _____

2. What Cross Reference Verse is God highlighting now? _____

_____
_____
_____

Prayerfully consider this new verse. What God is showing me in this Scripture:

About Work: _____

About Worship: _____

About Service: _____

In General: _____

3. What Cross Reference Verse is God highlighting now? _____

_____

_____

_____

Prayerfully consider this new verse. What God is showing me in this Scripture:

About Work: _____

About Worship: _____

About Service: _____

In General: _____

4. What Cross Reference Verse is God highlighting now? _____

_____

_____

_____

Prayerfully consider this new verse. What God is showing me in this Scripture:

About Work: _____

About Worship: _____

About Service: _____

In General: _____

Summarize Today's Treasure(s): _____

_____

_____

_____

_____

_____

Today's Declarations: _____

Today's Prayer: _____

When and how will I remind myself today? _____

Additional Notes:

AVADA Treasure Hunt

Day Ten. Date: _____

"I bless my spirit and I call it into the lead and grant it spiritual authority over my body and soul as I enter into this time with God and His Word."

I Praise God today for: _____

I Thank God today for: _____

1. Prayerfully Reflect on Today's Opening Verse: 1 Thessalonians 5:16-24

_____

_____

_____

What God is showing me in this Scripture:

About Work: _____

About Worship: _____

About Service: _____

In General: _____

2. What Cross Reference Verse is God highlighting now? _____

_____

_____

_____

Prayerfully consider this new verse. What God is showing me in this Scripture:

About Work: _____

About Worship: _____

About Service: _____

In General: _____

3. What Cross Reference Verse is God highlighting now? _____

_____

_____

_____

Prayerfully consider this new verse. What God is showing me in this Scripture:

About Work: _____

About Worship: _____

About Service: _____

In General: _____

4. What Cross Reference Verse is God highlighting now? _____

_____

_____

_____

Prayerfully consider this new verse. What God is showing me in this Scripture:

About Work: _____

About Worship: _____

About Service: _____

In General: _____

Summarize Today's Treasure(s): _____

_____

_____

_____

_____

_____

Today's Declarations: _____

Today's Prayer: _____

When and how will I remind myself today? _____

Additional Notes:

AVADA Treasure Hunt

Day Eleven. **Date:** _____

"I bless my spirit and I call it into the lead and grant it spiritual authority over my body and soul as I enter into this time with God and His Word."

I Praise God today for: _____

I Thank God today for: _____

1. Prayerfully Reflect on Today's Opening Verse: Psalm 24:1-5

_____
_____
_____

What God is showing me in this Scripture:

About Work: _____

About Worship: _____

About Service: _____

In General: _____

2. What Cross Reference Verse is God highlighting now? _____

_____
_____
_____

Prayerfully consider this new verse. What God is showing me in this Scripture:

About Work: _____

About Worship: _____

About Service: _____

In General: _____

3. What Cross Reference Verse is God highlighting now? _____

_____

_____

_____

Prayerfully consider this new verse. What God is showing me in this Scripture:

About Work: _____

About Worship: _____

About Service: _____

In General: _____

4. What Cross Reference Verse is God highlighting now? _____

_____

_____

_____

Prayerfully consider this new verse. What God is showing me in this Scripture:

About Work: _____

About Worship: _____

About Service: _____

In General: _____

Summarize Today's Treasure(s): _____

_____

_____

_____

_____

_____

Today's Declarations: _____

Today's Prayer: _____

When and how will I remind myself today? _____

Additional Notes:

AVADA Treasure Hunt

Day Twelve.   **Date:** _____

"I bless my spirit and I call it into the lead and grant it spiritual authority over my body and soul as I enter into this time with God and His Word."

I Praise God today for: _____

I Thank God today for: _____

1. Prayerfully Reflect on Today's Opening Verse: Ephesians 4:1-13

_____
_____
_____

What God is showing me in this Scripture:

About Work: _____

About Worship: _____

About Service: _____

In General: _____

2. What Cross Reference Verse is God highlighting now? _____

_____
_____
_____

Prayerfully consider this new verse. What God is showing me in this Scripture:

About Work: _____

About Worship: _____

About Service: _____

In General: _____

3. What Cross Reference Verse is God highlighting now? _____

_____

_____

_____

Prayerfully consider this new verse. What God is showing me in this Scripture:

About Work: _____

About Worship: _____

About Service: _____

In General: _____

4. What Cross Reference Verse is God highlighting now? _____

_____

_____

_____

Prayerfully consider this new verse. What God is showing me in this Scripture:

About Work: _____

About Worship: _____

About Service: _____

In General: _____

Summarize Today's Treasure(s): _____

_____

_____

_____

_____

_____

Today's Declarations: _____

Today's Prayer: _____

When and how will I remind myself today? _____

Additional Notes:

AVADA Treasure Hunt

Day Thirteen. Date: _____

"I bless my spirit and I call it into the lead and grant it spiritual authority over my body and soul as I enter into this time with God and His Word."

I Praise God today for: _____

I Thank God today for: _____

1. Prayerfully Reflect on Today's Opening Verse: 1 Timothy 6:3-10

_____
_____
_____

What God is showing me in this Scripture:

About Work: _____

About Worship: _____

About Service: _____

In General: _____

2. What Cross Reference Verse is God highlighting now? _____

_____
_____
_____

Prayerfully consider this new verse. What God is showing me in this Scripture:

About Work: _____

About Worship: _____

About Service: _____

In General: _____

3. What Cross Reference Verse is God highlighting now? _____

_____

_____

_____

Prayerfully consider this new verse. What God is showing me in this Scripture:

About Work: _____

About Worship: _____

About Service: _____

In General: _____

4. What Cross Reference Verse is God highlighting now? _____

_____

_____

_____

Prayerfully consider this new verse. What God is showing me in this Scripture:

About Work: _____

About Worship: _____

About Service: _____

In General: _____

Summarize Today's Treasure(s): _____

_____

_____

_____

_____

_____

Today's Declarations: _____

Today's Prayer: _____

When and how will I remind myself today? _____

Additional Notes:

The AVADA™ Life Treasure Hunt

AVADA Treasure Hunt

Day Fourteen. **Date:** _____

"I bless my spirit and I call it into the lead and grant it spiritual authority over my body and soul as I enter into this time with God and His Word."

I Praise God today for: _____

I Thank God today for: _____

1. Prayerfully Reflect on Today's Opening Verse: John 15:12-17

_____
_____
_____

What God is showing me in this Scripture:

About Work: _____

About Worship: _____

About Service: _____

In General: _____

2. What Cross Reference Verse is God highlighting now? _____

_____
_____
_____

Prayerfully consider this new verse. What God is showing me in this Scripture:

About Work: _____

About Worship: _____

About Service: _____

In General: _____

3. What Cross Reference Verse is God highlighting now? _____
_____
_____
_____

Prayerfully consider this new verse. What God is showing me in this Scripture:

About Work: _____

About Worship: _____

About Service: _____

In General: _____

4. What Cross Reference Verse is God highlighting now? _____
_____
_____
_____

Prayerfully consider this new verse. What God is showing me in this Scripture:

About Work: _____

About Worship: _____

About Service: _____

In General: _____

Summarize Today's Treasure(s): _____

_____

_____

_____

_____

_____

Today's Declarations: _____

Today's Prayer: _____

When and how will I remind myself today? _____

Additional Notes:

AVADA Treasure Hunt

Day Fifteen.   Date: _____

"I bless my spirit and I call it into the lead and grant it spiritual authority over my body and soul as I enter into this time with God and His Word."

I Praise God today for: _____

I Thank God today for: _____

1. Prayerfully Reflect on Today's Opening Verse: Matthew 28:16-20

_____
_____
_____

What God is showing me in this Scripture:

About Work: _____

About Worship: _____

About Service: _____

In General: _____

2. What Cross Reference Verse is God highlighting now? _____

_____
_____
_____

Prayerfully consider this new verse. What God is showing me in this Scripture:

About Work: _____

About Worship: _____

About Service: _____

In General: _____

3. What Cross Reference Verse is God highlighting now? _____

_____

_____

_____

Prayerfully consider this new verse. What God is showing me in this Scripture:

About Work: _____

About Worship: _____

About Service: _____

In General: _____

4. What Cross Reference Verse is God highlighting now? _____

_____

_____

_____

Prayerfully consider this new verse. What God is showing me in this Scripture:

About Work: _____

About Worship: _____

About Service: _____

In General: _____

Summarize Today's Treasure(s): _____

_____

_____

_____

_____

_____

Today's Declarations: _____

Today's Prayer: _____

When and how will I remind myself today? _____

Additional Notes:

AVADA Treasure Hunt

Day Sixteen. Date: _____

"I bless my spirit and I call it into the lead and grant it spiritual authority over my body and soul as I enter into this time with God and His Word."

I Praise God today for: _____

I Thank God today for: _____

1. Prayerfully Reflect on Today's Opening Verse: Psalm 115:1-8

_____

_____

_____

What God is showing me in this Scripture:

About Work: _____

About Worship: _____

About Service: _____

In General: _____

2. What Cross Reference Verse is God highlighting now? _____

_____

_____

_____

Prayerfully consider this new verse. What God is showing me in this Scripture:

About Work: _____

About Worship: _____

About Service: _____

In General: _____

3. What Cross Reference Verse is God highlighting now? _____

_____

_____

_____

Prayerfully consider this new verse. What God is showing me in this Scripture:

About Work: _____

About Worship: _____

About Service: _____

In General: _____

4. What Cross Reference Verse is God highlighting now? _____

_____

_____

_____

Prayerfully consider this new verse. What God is showing me in this Scripture:

About Work: _____

About Worship: _____

About Service: _____

In General: _____

Summarize Today's Treasure(s): _____

_____

_____

_____

_____

_____

Today's Declarations: _____

Today's Prayer: _____

When and how will I remind myself today? _____

Additional Notes:

AVADA Treasure Hunt

Day Seventeen. Date: _____

"I bless my spirit and I call it into the lead and grant it spiritual authority over my body and soul as I enter into this time with God and His Word."

I Praise God today for: _____

I Thank God today for: _____

1. Prayerfully Reflect on Today's Opening Verse: Mark 12:38-44

_____
_____
_____

What God is showing me in this Scripture:

About Work: _____

About Worship: _____

About Service: _____

In General: _____

2. What Cross Reference Verse is God highlighting now? _____

_____
_____
_____

Prayerfully consider this new verse. What God is showing me in this Scripture:

About Work: _____

About Worship: _____

About Service: _____

In General: _____

3. What Cross Reference Verse is God highlighting now? _____

_____

_____

_____

Prayerfully consider this new verse. What God is showing me in this Scripture:

About Work: _____

About Worship: _____

About Service: _____

In General: _____

4. What Cross Reference Verse is God highlighting now? _____

_____

_____

_____

Prayerfully consider this new verse. What God is showing me in this Scripture:

About Work: _____

About Worship: _____

About Service: _____

In General: _____

Summarize Today's Treasure(s): _____

_____

_____

_____

_____

_____

Today's Declarations: _____

Today's Prayer: _____

When and how will I remind myself today? _____

Additional Notes:

AVADA TREASURE HUNT

Day Eighteen.   **Date:** _____

"I bless my spirit and I call it into the lead and grant it spiritual authority over my body and soul as I enter into this time with God and His Word."

I Praise God today for: _____

I Thank God today for: _____

1. Prayerfully Reflect on Today's Opening Verse: John 4:21-28

_____

_____

_____

What God is showing me in this Scripture:

About Work: _____

About Worship: _____

About Service: _____

In General: _____

2. What Cross Reference Verse is God highlighting now? _____

_____

_____

_____

Prayerfully consider this new verse. What God is showing me in this Scripture:

About Work: _____

About Worship: _____

About Service: _____

In General: _____

3. What Cross Reference Verse is God highlighting now? _____

_____

_____

_____

Prayerfully consider this new verse. What God is showing me in this Scripture:

About Work: _____

About Worship: _____

About Service: _____

In General: _____

4. What Cross Reference Verse is God highlighting now? _____

_____

_____

_____

Prayerfully consider this new verse. What God is showing me in this Scripture:

About Work: _____

About Worship: _____

About Service: _____

In General: _____

Summarize Today's Treasure(s): _____

_____

_____

_____

_____

_____

Today's Declarations: _____

Today's Prayer: _____

When and how will I remind myself today? _____

Additional Notes:

AVADA Treasure Hunt

Day Nineteen.   Date: _____

"I bless my spirit and I call it into the lead and grant it spiritual authority over my body and soul as I enter into this time with God and His Word."

I Praise God today for: _____

I Thank God today for: _____

1. Prayerfully Reflect on Today's Opening Verse: Exodus 32:1-6

_____

_____

_____

What God is showing me in this Scripture:

About Work: _____

About Worship: _____

About Service: _____

In General: _____

2. What Cross Reference Verse is God highlighting now? _____

_____

_____

_____

Prayerfully consider this new verse. What God is showing me in this Scripture:

About Work: _____

About Worship: _____

About Service: _____

In General: _____

3. What Cross Reference Verse is God highlighting now? _____

_____

_____

_____

Prayerfully consider this new verse. What God is showing me in this Scripture:

About Work: _____

About Worship: _____

About Service: _____

In General: _____

4. What Cross Reference Verse is God highlighting now? _____

_____

_____

_____

Prayerfully consider this new verse. What God is showing me in this Scripture:

About Work: _____

About Worship: _____

About Service: _____

In General: _____

Summarize Today's Treasure(s): _____

_____

_____

_____

_____

_____

Today's Declarations: _____

Today's Prayer: _____

When and how will I remind myself today? _____

Additional Notes:

AVADA TREASURE HUNT

Day Twenty. **Date:** _____

"I bless my spirit and I call it into the lead and grant it spiritual authority over my body and soul as I enter into this time with God and His Word."

I Praise God today for: _____

I Thank God today for: _____

1. Prayerfully Reflect on Today's Opening Verse: James 1:22-27

_____

_____

_____

What God is showing me in this Scripture:

About Work: _____

About Worship: _____

About Service: _____

In General: _____

2. What Cross Reference Verse is God highlighting now? _____

_____

_____

_____

Prayerfully consider this new verse. What God is showing me in this Scripture:

About Work: _____

About Worship: _____

About Service: _____

In General: _____

3. What Cross Reference Verse is God highlighting now? _____

_____

_____

_____

Prayerfully consider this new verse. What God is showing me in this Scripture:

About Work: _____

About Worship: _____

About Service: _____

In General: _____

4. What Cross Reference Verse is God highlighting now? _____

_____

_____

_____

Prayerfully consider this new verse. What God is showing me in this Scripture:

About Work: _____

About Worship: _____

About Service: _____

In General: _____

Summarize Today's Treasure(s): _____

_____

_____

_____

_____

_____

Today's Declarations: _____

Today's Prayer: _____

When and how will I remind myself today? _____

Additional Notes:

AVADA Treasure Hunt

Day Twenty One. Date: _____

"I bless my spirit and I call it into the lead and grant it spiritual authority over my body and soul as I enter into this time with God and His Word."

I Praise God today for: _____

I Thank God today for: _____

1. Prayerfully Reflect on Today's Opening Verse: Psalm 37:1-9

_____
_____
_____

What God is showing me in this Scripture:

About Work: _____

About Worship: _____

About Service: _____

In General: _____

2. What Cross Reference Verse is God highlighting now? _____

_____
_____
_____

Prayerfully consider this new verse. What God is showing me in this Scripture:

About Work: _____

About Worship: _____

About Service: _____

In General: _____

3. What Cross Reference Verse is God highlighting now? _____

_____

_____

_____

Prayerfully consider this new verse. What God is showing me in this Scripture:

About Work: _____

About Worship: _____

About Service: _____

In General: _____

4. What Cross Reference Verse is God highlighting now? _____

_____

_____

_____

Prayerfully consider this new verse. What God is showing me in this Scripture:

About Work: _____

About Worship: _____

About Service: _____

In General: _____

Summarize Today's Treasure(s): _____

_____

_____

_____

_____

_____

Today's Declarations: _____

Today's Prayer: _____

When and how will I remind myself today? _____

Additional Notes:

AVADA TREASURE HUNT

Day Twenty Two. **Date:** _____

"I bless my spirit and I call it into the lead and grant it spiritual authority over my body and soul as I enter into this time with God and His Word."

I Praise God today for: _____

I Thank God today for: _____

1. Prayerfully Reflect on Today's Opening Verse: Deuteronomy 8:10-19

_____

_____

_____

What God is showing me in this Scripture:

About Work: _____

About Worship: _____

About Service: _____

In General: _____

2. What Cross Reference Verse is God highlighting now? _____

_____

_____

_____

Prayerfully consider this new verse. What God is showing me in this Scripture:

About Work: _____

About Worship: _____

About Service: _____

In General: _____

3. What Cross Reference Verse is God highlighting now? _____

_____

_____

Prayerfully consider this new verse. What God is showing me in this Scripture:

About Work: _____

About Worship: _____

About Service: _____

In General: _____

4. What Cross Reference Verse is God highlighting now? _____

_____

_____

Prayerfully consider this new verse. What God is showing me in this Scripture:

About Work: _____

About Worship: _____

About Service: _____

In General: _____

Summarize Today's Treasure(s): _____

_____

_____

_____

_____

_____

Today's Declarations: _____

Today's Prayer: _____

When and how will I remind myself today? _____

Additional Notes:

AVADA Treasure Hunt

Day Twenty Three.   **Date:** _____

"I bless my spirit and I call it into the lead and grant it spiritual authority over my body and soul as I enter into this time with God and His Word."

I Praise God today for: _____

I Thank God today for: _____

1. Prayerfully Reflect on Today's Opening Verse: Psalm 100:1-5

_____

_____

_____

What God is showing me in this Scripture:

About Work: _____

About Worship: _____

About Service: _____

In General: _____

2. What Cross Reference Verse is God highlighting now? _____

_____

_____

_____

Prayerfully consider this new verse. What God is showing me in this Scripture:

About Work: _____

About Worship: _____

About Service: _____

In General: _____

3. What Cross Reference Verse is God highlighting now? _____

_____

_____

_____

Prayerfully consider this new verse. What God is showing me in this Scripture:

About Work: _____

About Worship: _____

About Service: _____

In General: _____

4. What Cross Reference Verse is God highlighting now? _____

_____

_____

_____

Prayerfully consider this new verse. What God is showing me in this Scripture:

About Work: _____

About Worship: _____

About Service: _____

In General: _____

Summarize Today's Treasure(s): _____

_____

_____

_____

_____

_____

Today's Declarations: _____

Today's Prayer: _____

When and how will I remind myself today? _____

Additional Notes:

AVADA TREASURE HUNT

Day Twenty Four. Date: _____

"I bless my spirit and I call it into the lead and grant it spiritual authority over my body and soul as I enter into this time with God and His Word."

I Praise God today for: _____

I Thank God today for: _____

1. Prayerfully Reflect on Today's Opening Verse: 1 Corinthians 12:4-11

_____
_____
_____

What God is showing me in this Scripture:

About Work: _____

About Worship: _____

About Service: _____

In General: _____

2. What Cross Reference Verse is God highlighting now? _____

_____
_____
_____

Prayerfully consider this new verse. What God is showing me in this Scripture:

About Work: _____

About Worship: _____

About Service: _____

In General: _____

3. What Cross Reference Verse is God highlighting now? _____

_____

_____

Prayerfully consider this new verse. What God is showing me in this Scripture:

About Work: _____

About Worship: _____

About Service: _____

In General: _____

4. What Cross Reference Verse is God highlighting now? _____

_____

_____

Prayerfully consider this new verse. What God is showing me in this Scripture:

About Work: _____

About Worship: _____

About Service: _____

In General: _____

Summarize Today's Treasure(s): _____

_____

_____

_____

_____

_____

Today's Declarations: _____

Today's Prayer: _____

When and how will I remind myself today? _____

Additional Notes:

AVADA Treasure Hunt

Day Twenty Five.   Date: _____

"I bless my spirit and I call it into the lead and grant it spiritual authority over my body and soul as I enter into this time with God and His Word."

I Praise God today for: _____

I Thank God today for: _____

1. Prayerfully Reflect on Today's Opening Verse: Matthew 20:20-28

_____

_____

_____

What God is showing me in this Scripture:

About Work: _____

About Worship: _____

About Service: _____

In General: _____

2. What Cross Reference Verse is God highlighting now? _____

_____

_____

_____

Prayerfully consider this new verse. What God is showing me in this Scripture:

About Work: _____

About Worship: _____

About Service: _____

In General: _____

3. What Cross Reference Verse is God highlighting now? _____

_____

_____

_____

Prayerfully consider this new verse. What God is showing me in this Scripture:

About Work: _____

About Worship: _____

About Service: _____

In General: _____

4. What Cross Reference Verse is God highlighting now? _____

_____

_____

_____

Prayerfully consider this new verse. What God is showing me in this Scripture:

About Work: _____

About Worship: _____

About Service: _____

In General: _____

Summarize Today's Treasure(s): _____
_____
_____
_____
_____
_____

Today's Declarations: _____

Today's Prayer: _____

When and how will I remind myself today? _____

Additional Notes:

AVADA Treasure Hunt

Day Twenty Six.   **Date:** _____

"I bless my spirit and I call it into the lead and grant it spiritual authority over my body and soul as I enter into this time with God and His Word."

I Praise God today for: _____

I Thank God today for: _____

1. Prayerfully Reflect on Today's Opening Verse: Psalm 8:1,3-6

_____

_____

_____

What God is showing me in this Scripture:

About Work: _____

About Worship: _____

About Service: _____

In General: _____

2. What Cross Reference Verse is God highlighting now? _____

_____

_____

_____

Prayerfully consider this new verse. What God is showing me in this Scripture:

About Work: _____

About Worship: _____

About Service: _____

In General: _____

3. What Cross Reference Verse is God highlighting now? _____
_____
_____
_____

Prayerfully consider this new verse. What God is showing me in this Scripture:

About Work: _____

About Worship: _____

About Service: _____

In General: _____

4. What Cross Reference Verse is God highlighting now? _____
_____
_____
_____

Prayerfully consider this new verse. What God is showing me in this Scripture:

About Work: _____

About Worship: _____

About Service: _____

In General: _____

Summarize Today's Treasure(s): _____

_____

_____

_____

_____

_____

Today's Declarations: _____

Today's Prayer: _____

When and how will I remind myself today? _____

Additional Notes:

AVADA Treasure Hunt

Day Twenty Seven. Date: _____

"I bless my spirit and I call it into the lead and grant it spiritual authority over my body and soul as I enter into this time with God and His Word."

I Praise God today for: _____

I Thank God today for: _____

1. Prayerfully Reflect on Today's Opening Verse: 2 Corinthians 5:15-21

_____

_____

_____

What God is showing me in this Scripture:

About Work: _____

About Worship: _____

About Service: _____

In General: _____

2. What Cross Reference Verse is God highlighting now? _____

_____

_____

_____

Prayerfully consider this new verse. What God is showing me in this Scripture:

About Work: _____

About Worship: _____

About Service: _____

In General: _____

3. What Cross Reference Verse is God highlighting now? _____

_____

_____

_____

Prayerfully consider this new verse. What God is showing me in this Scripture:

About Work: _____

About Worship: _____

About Service: _____

In General: _____

4. What Cross Reference Verse is God highlighting now? _____

_____

_____

_____

Prayerfully consider this new verse. What God is showing me in this Scripture:

About Work: _____

About Worship: _____

About Service: _____

In General: _____

Summarize Today's Treasure(s): _____

_____

_____

_____

_____

_____

Today's Declarations: _____

Today's Prayer: _____

When and how will I remind myself today? _____

Additional Notes:

AVADA TREASURE HUNT

Day Twenty Eight. Date: _____

"I bless my spirit and I call it into the lead and grant it spiritual authority over my body and soul as I enter into this time with God and His Word."

I Praise God today for: _____

I Thank God today for: _____

1. Prayerfully Reflect on Today's Opening Verse: James 3:3-6, 9-12

_____
_____
_____

What God is showing me in this Scripture:

About Work: _____

About Worship: _____

About Service: _____

In General: _____

2. What Cross Reference Verse is God highlighting now? _____

_____
_____
_____

Prayerfully consider this new verse. What God is showing me in this Scripture:

About Work: _____

About Worship: _____

About Service: _____

In General: _____

3. What Cross Reference Verse is God highlighting now? _____

_____

_____

Prayerfully consider this new verse. What God is showing me in this Scripture:

About Work: _____

About Worship: _____

About Service: _____

In General: _____

4. What Cross Reference Verse is God highlighting now? _____

_____

_____

Prayerfully consider this new verse. What God is showing me in this Scripture:

About Work: _____

About Worship: _____

About Service: _____

In General: _____

Summarize Today's Treasure(s): _____

_____

_____

_____

_____

_____

Today's Declarations: _____

Today's Prayer: _____

When and how will I remind myself today? _____

Additional Notes:

AVADA Treasure Hunt

Day Twenty Nine. Date: _____

"I bless my spirit and I call it into the lead and grant it spiritual authority over my body and soul as I enter into this time with God and His Word."

I Praise God today for: _____

I Thank God today for: _____

1. Prayerfully Reflect on Today's Opening Verse: Ephesians 6:10-18

_____

_____

_____

What God is showing me in this Scripture:

About Work: _____

About Worship: _____

About Service: _____

In General: _____

2. What Cross Reference Verse is God highlighting now? _____

_____

_____

_____

Prayerfully consider this new verse. What God is showing me in this Scripture:

About Work: _____

About Worship: _____

About Service: _____

In General: _____

3. What Cross Reference Verse is God highlighting now? _____

_____

_____

_____

Prayerfully consider this new verse. What God is showing me in this Scripture:

About Work: _____

About Worship: _____

About Service: _____

In General: _____

4. What Cross Reference Verse is God highlighting now? _____

_____

_____

_____

Prayerfully consider this new verse. What God is showing me in this Scripture:

About Work: _____

About Worship: _____

About Service: _____

In General: _____

Summarize Today's Treasure(s): _____

_____

_____

_____

_____

_____

Today's Declarations: _____

Today's Prayer: _____

When and how will I remind myself today? _____

Additional Notes:

AVADA Treasure Hunt

Day Thirty. **Date:** _____

"I bless my spirit and I call it into the lead and grant it spiritual authority over my body and soul as I enter into this time with God and His Word."

I Praise God today for: _____

I Thank God today for: _____

1. Prayerfully Reflect on Today's Opening Verse: Galatians 5:16-25

_____

_____

_____

What God is showing me in this Scripture:

About Work: _____

About Worship: _____

About Service: _____

In General: _____

2. What Cross Reference Verse is God highlighting now? _____

_____

_____

_____

Prayerfully consider this new verse. What God is showing me in this Scripture:

About Work: _____

About Worship: _____

About Service: _____

In General: _____

3. What Cross Reference Verse is God highlighting now? _____

_____

_____

Prayerfully consider this new verse. What God is showing me in this Scripture:

About Work: _____

About Worship: _____

About Service: _____

In General: _____

4. What Cross Reference Verse is God highlighting now? _____

_____

_____

Prayerfully consider this new verse. What God is showing me in this Scripture:

About Work: _____

About Worship: _____

About Service: _____

In General: _____

Summarize Today's Treasure(s): _____

_____

_____

_____

_____

_____

Today's Declarations: _____

Today's Prayer: _____

When and how will I remind myself today? _____

Additional Notes:

Conclusion

Congratulations! I expect you have much Treasure to show for your diligence over the last 30 days. Now that you have learned how to study this way, I encourage you to return to the methodology frequently. Choose a word or a topic. Using Google or a Bible reference, let God highlight a verse to start with and launch your Treasure Hunt.

Closing Prayer:

Father, thank you for the revelation of the AVADA Principle. Thank you for your promise that you will breathe blessing and favor on us as we pursue an integrated life of work toward your purposes, worship in your presence, and service in your power.

I pray for the reader of this Workbook right now and for everyone who hears the AVADA message that you give them the passion, wisdom, courage, and strength to:

Desire you and seek you with every fiber of their being.

Receive your Presence and your Holy Spirit.

Embrace your Holy Spirit and the gifts of the Spirit you so graciously give.

Use and experience those gifts fully in the power you provide.

Continually enjoy and delight in your presence.

Love you with all their spirit, mind, and body and then love others likewise.

Fulfill the Great Commission in the capacity you have for them.

Model your love to the world through how they love others.

Live an integrated life of work, worship, and service in every aspect of their lives—24 hours a day, seven days a week, 365 days a year for the rest of their lives and for all eternity.

Father, I pray that you bring your shalom peace to them, in the fullest sense of the word, as they pursue an AVADA Life.

Finally, I pray that as they live an AVADA Life that they are blessed by receiving the fruit of Your Spirit, which is love, joy, peace, forbearance, kindness, goodness, faithfulness, gentleness and self-control.

I pray these things in the most Holy Name of the Lord Jesus Christ.

May it be so.

Additional Resources

➤ The AVADA Life Webinar Series

➤ The AVADA Life Independent Licensing Program for those who would like to coach others in an AVADA Life

➤ For more information on these resources, visit www.10xGroups.com/AVADA

➤ To arrange for Michael Sipe to speak to your organization or keynote at an event, or to discuss custom seminars and workshops, contact him at:

AVADAPublishing@gmail.com

www.10xGroups.com

About the Author

Michael Sipe is an ex-Army Ranger Captain, entrepreneur, mergers and acquisitions advisor and Christian executive coach. He's founded, bought and sold multiple companies for his own account. As an investment banker, in the last 30 years he's evaluated over 5,000 businesses in about every industry conceivable; and provided advisory services for approximately half a billion dollars in business sales involving hundreds of companies. Since 2013, he's facilitated Christian CEO roundtable forums in which members meet monthly in small peer groups to focus on spiritual growth as leaders, business excellence and marketplace ministry using the platform of their businesses. He serves as an executive coach to extremely successful business leaders, many in the top 1% of income earners in the United States. A consistent theme in his life and in that of his clients is the quest for an abundant life of significance and meaning. He, and they, desire not only a full, properly ordered and well-balanced life, but more importantly, an integrated life that glorifies God; while leading with excellence in the marketplace as men and women of faith called to run exceptional businesses. The AVADA Principle and this book is the fruit of that quest.

You can reach Michael at **AVADAPublishing@gmail.com** or **www.10xgroups.com**.

Made in the USA
Monee, IL
01 May 2023